A COMMUNITY COLLABORATION

MM
PUBLICATION

VOLUME 00

SUMMER/FALL 2023

MM Publication Vol. 00
June 2023

Director of Publications
Kristen Rud

Lead Editor
Sharissa Bradley

Creative Director
Tia Ellington

Contributors:
Kristen Rud
Tanya Murguia
Riss Magdalena
Tia Esther
Heather Lukacs
Jaime Phillips
Summer Whiteside
Charis Gaston
Nicole Giordano
Lacey Wynn
Stori Nagel
Liz Funk
Alicia Richardson
Pamela Buehl
Tracy Herzog
Dede Jones
Christina Sanders
Roxanne Johns
Jesse St James
Vivianna Severance
Moira Jamey Flora
Adriane Alvarez
Ashley Llano
Claire Schembri
Isabel Cuevas
Alisha Meyer
Megan Masler
Sarah Becerra
Victoria Rodomista
Jennifer Ramos
Sharissa Bradley
Brock Bertloff
Alyssa VanDerLinden
Liana Soria

Sales, Subscriptions & Submissions
www.mmpublication.org
kristen@mermaidmovement.online

Maiden to Mother to Crone

As a community, we are dedicated to serving and supporting women through birth, rebirth and the sacred rites of passage in their lives. We strive to flow between ancient wisdom and practical, evidence-based tools to create a culture that is conducive to wellness and growth.

Reaching women allows us to reach the entire family unit, the entire community. Our 'woman-at-the-center' approach allows our mission to ripple throughout households and lineages.

Seasonal Living

Slowly, as a society, we are questioning the cultural constructs that are generally accepted as truth and re-discovering a variety of repressed histories of women's wellbeing.

Uncovering the web of dis-ease in women really starts with the cultural beliefs and expectations placed upon women to uphold a linear lifestyle with a cyclical design.

We envision these artistic and informative publications on coffee tables and shelves as a guide to a post-modern women's lifestyle in the 2020s and beyond.

Why do Women's Stories Matter?

"For centuries, storytelling has connected individuals to their communities' history. In traditional cultures, this led to stories that explain the origins of the first people and everything in the natural world, including what brings rain and what makes the sun rise and set. There are teaching stories about planting, herding, weaving, getting along with others, healing, dying- and about birthing. Before initiates undertook a rite of passage or a vision quest, stories informed them about what to eat and drink, how to find herbs for healing, and landmarks to look for to ensure completion of their personal tasks."

-Pam England, Ancient Map for Modern Birth

INSPIRATION FOR THE MODERN MAGDALENA

MM

Highlights

Table of Contents

AN AYURVEDIC VIEW TO A BALANCED YEAR

BY TANYA MURGUIA,
NOURISH & RENEW

Do you ever feel out of sync with nature and out of balance with the seasons? *Ayurveda*, an ancient Indian holistic healing system, can help you regain that connection to nature and its seasons.

There are five elements: *space, air, fire, water,* and *earth*. These 5 elements are grouped into 3 doshas called *Vata, Pitta,* and *Kapha*. These doshas are reflected in our bodies, our seasons, and so much more!

Adjust meals, routines, and exercise to maintain balance in your mind, body, and spirit throughout the year by knowing which dosha is dominate in that season.

Scan the QR Code to connect with Tanya!

DISCOVER YOUR DOSHA

01 What animal best represents your physical body?

    A. Deer
    B. Tiger
    C. Elephant

02 How do you handle stress?

    A. Take a walk outside
    B. Tackle tasks one-by-one
    C. Curl up on the couch with a good book or movie

03 How do you feel about change?

    A. Excited! I love trying new things
    B. It depends on the situation
    C. I prefer stability and routine

04 What's your favorite type of exercise?

    A. Yoga or stretching
    B. High-intensity cardio or weight lifting
    C. Low-impact activities like walking or swimming

05 Where would you love to live?

    A. In the hot dry desert
    B. In a hot and humid tropical rainforest
    C. In the cool forest mountains

06 What's your skin type?

    A. Dry or rough
    B. Sensitive or prone to inflammation
    C. Oily or prone to congestion

READY TO FIND OUT YOUR MAGICAL POWERS?!

Take this quiz to reveal your special elemental blend of **natural-born magic** so you can become even more **powerful** and **balanced**.

07 How do you approach your work or hobbies?

    A. With creativity and spontaneity
    B. With organization and structure
    C. With consistency and dedication

08 What is your favorite season?

    A. Fall or winter
    B. Summer
    C. Spring

09 What do you do when confronted with conflict?

    A. I avoid it. Run away.
    B. I will not get pushed around, I fight back.
    C. Why so angry? I try to come up with a common ground and make peace.

10 What are your dreams like?

    A. Don't remember; lots of traveling, flying, running or jumping
    B. More violent and fighting
    C. Love stories; more water and clouds

YOUR DOSHA DISCOVERED

MOSTLY A'S - VATA'S MAGICAL **POWERS OF THE CREATIVE HEALER.**

MOSTLY B'S - PITTA'S MAGICAL **POWERS OF THE LEADING WARRIOR**

MOSTLY C'S - KAPHA'S MAGICAL **POWER OF THE LOVING PROTECTOR**

Remember, this quiz is just a fun way to discover your dosha tendencies. Consult with an Ayurvedic coach for personalized recommendations on how to support your unique mind-body type!

AYURVEDA
& THE SEASONS

"Feminine energy is cyclic. We flow with nature, moving through hormonal fluctuations with the moon. Transforming from maiden to mother to crone- again and again and again- like the life in your garden.

The Wheel of the Year guided our ancestors who lived in accordance with nature. The Wheel of the Woman reconnects us to this rhythm. Ayurveda is the ancient science that gives meaning to these cycles.

These wheels give us a visual representation of our true connection to one another through nature."

-Kristen Rud

SEASONAL TIPS
FROM TANYA

1. PITTA
SUMMER

- Stay cool and hydrated.
- Avoid spicy, oily, and acidic foods.
- Practice relaxation techniques like meditation and deep breathing.
- Spend time near water.

2. VATA
FALL & EARLY WINTER

- Stay warm and hydrated.
- Avoid cold and dry foods.
- Practice grounding activities like yoga or walking in nature.

3. KAPHA
LATE WINTER & SPRING

- Get plenty of sunlight and fresh air.
- Avoid heavy, oily, and sweet foods.
- Practice stimulating activities like high-intensity exercise and dry brushing.
- Focus on detoxifying foods and herbs.

KNOWING EARTH IS HAVING *FREEDOM*: *a love letter to the earth*

BY RISS MAGDALENA

The idea that we, or any individual species rather, can control, change, or improve Earth is comical at best. Human exceptionalism is crumbled by the tearing of this veil. Earth's mastery of shape shifting as it cycles in and out of diverse phases is completely unstirred by human will, and absolutely enchanting might I add. Witnessing wild plants and animals embody and align to Earth's phases with intrinsic rhythms that intelligently guide them through time and place will leave you awestruck. The sensation of relief seeps into your being and frees you. Desire for control becomes laughable. Your wild kin not only surrender but depend on embodiment of Earth's rhythms; Why as a fellow Earth being would it be different for you?

I must admit, I still cry when I drive down a hill and see Earth's land out of alignment, but I am freed. Rooting in my place and knowing Earth by relationship makes me feel insignificant in the holiest of ways. May we all be at peace with the inevitable fact that refusal to dwell with Earth will lead to our own extinction. I sorrowfully honor all the species we have and will destroy because of our enslavement to human exceptionalism and I know one day again Earth will be prolific with beings that live harmoniously with her cycles. After we are gone, Earth will be steady as ever: Winter will turn into Spring, the ocean tides with rise and fall, and day and night will continue to cycle. **We are free.**

PART TWO TO FOLLOW IN THE NEXT MM PUBLICATION.

PART ONE

As a child, I cried in the backseat of the car anytime we climbed in elevation and saw city views out the window. I'd sense: 'What an ugly scar over what should be earth's natural expression.' I had the utmost reverence and empathy for Earth and all Earth Beings. However, my shallow understanding of Earth held me captive in many ways. If I wanted the Earth to thrive, the weight was on my shoulders. Even for myself to thrive, it would be a lifelong journey of muscling my way to success. It wasn't until years later, when I stopped perceiving Earth and began communing with her that I began to deeply know her. I became graciously humbled and vigorously freed.

Scan the QR Code to connect with Riss

CHAT WITH TIA ESTHER CREATIVE

Q: *Did you always know you wanted to be a photographer?*

A: I grew up in Anza, Ca , a small town with not very much to do. I took to cameras at a young age. Taking photos of my stuffed animals, plants, weeds and anything else that caught my eye with a disposable camera. As I grew older and got into school, I didn't play with my cameras as much. Being a social butterfly was much more important at the time. It wasn't until high school that I decided to play with cameras again. I would take my point and shoot to football games, cheer and dance practices and basically everywhere. My junior year, I moved in with my dad and he gave me his Rebel series Canon DSLR. I used it through out the rest of my high school career but by the time I graduated in 2011 and moved, it took a back seat again.

Q: *What made you move back behind the lens?*

A: In 2015, my dad unexpectedly passed away and I couldn't help but hear him over and over when it came to my camera... "If I give this to you, you'd better do something with it". There were so few recent photos of my dad and I.. it sparked something inside of me to pick up my camera again and so I did and never looked back.

Q: *How did you get started?*

I built my business while working a 9-5 for five years and finally in 2020 I quit my job to go full-time into photography and it was the best decision I could've made for my business. I've been working my business ever since and it is the greatest passion for me to be involved in so many incredible journeys while getting to document it for generations to come. Photos, to me, are the most valuable memoirs you can pass down to your loved ones.

Q: *What is your mission now?*

My business is now based in Temecula, Ca but I travel a lot and love to do so, meeting new people and getting to be in so many different environments. This allows for constant creative power and passion. Hence the name, Tia Esther Creative.

Q: *Any advice for aspiring photographers and creatives?*

I would tell them to never give up on the process. Fall in love with ***the process*** as much as you do your business or passion. Remember that there is enough business to go around and that your faith in your business will be what keeps it going. Keep your community close to support you in trying times and know that you're never alone, and the life you want is just some hard work away.

Scan the QR Code to connect with Tia

"I was never taught how to love myself."

TIA ESTHER PHOTOGRAPHY

JOURNEY TO SELF LOVE
BY *HEATHER LUKACS*

I remember being the insecure girl. I remember being the chubby girl. I wanted everyone's approval. I wanted to be liked, and for people to think I was beautiful. I craved that feeling. I needed it. I remember feeling rejected.

Ever since I was little, I wanted to change my appearance in order to fit the idea of beauty that I had created inside my head. I wanted longer hair, a smaller stomach, smoother skin, and everything in between. I wanted to look like the other girls around me because I thought it would make people like me.

Connect with Heather on Instagram

A few years ago I decided to change myself. Not on the outside! I decided to change my mind. I decided to see myself as the beautiful woman I am. I decided that I loved my body. And that's that. A simple concept albeit with an arduous journey of completion.

It has taken me more than 30 years to realize that I wasn't seeking approval from others. I was really seeking approval – and love – from myself. I didn't love myself. I was never taught how to. In retrospect, I wasn't taught how to hate myself either but I somehow had that ingrained into my brain before I even knew how to ride a bike.

This takes daily, intentional work. I went to Spiritual Summer Camp. I met women who were vastly different from me yet were also on similar journeys. I intentionally seek out positive books, podcasts, social media accounts, and other humans who make me feel good about myself.

I still struggle with this all the time. However, when I'm having a hard time, I go back to my decision to love myself. I remember that this will be a forever journey for me. Some days are hard and some days are easy – both are important. Life is unequivocally what you make it – and I want to make mine as beautiful as possible. Both inside my head and in reality.

3 Tips for Every Holistic Pet Mama

By Jaime Phillips

1. FOOD ENERGETICS

Does your pet have itchy, inflamed skin? Consider switching their protein source in their diet to a "cooling" protein. Traditional Chinese Medicine's food energetics chart categorizes every meat into warm, neutral, or cool in terms of how it affects the body. If your pet is currently on a "warm" protein (such as chicken, beef, venison, or salmon), and experiencing itchy, red, inflamed skin, try switching their food to a "cooling" protein (such as duck, rabbit, or even pork) to help ease inflammation.

2. FLEA + TICK PREVENTION

Common flea and tick control products and "medicines" are extremely toxic and contribute to alarming issues such as neurological damage, paralysis, and even death, as they are quite literally chemical pesticides being placed into your pet's bloodstream. Consider switching to topical herbal-based preventative sprays and shampoos from brands such as Cedarcide, Wondercide, and Kin+Kind.

3. BIOLOGICALLY APPROPRIATE DIET

Most commercial pet foods on the market contain cheap filler ingredients to help keep the cost of the food down. However our pets do not biologically produce enough amylase in their saliva, like we humans do, to properly break down complex starches such as potatoes, grains, and legumes. Buildup of these ingredients in your pet's system over time leads to a multitude of issues including yeast overgrowth and ear infections. Look for foods that exclude potatoes (even sweet potatoes), first and foremost. Better yet - ditch the processed kibbles and canned foods altogether, and make the switch to a species-appropriate, raw, meat-based diet.

Vitamin Infusions by the Season

Summer:

I recommend getting a vitamin C infusion for its ability to help heal the skin from all of the strong UV rays from the summer sun. I also recommend B12 shots for the long days since it aids in metabolizing the nutrients your cells need to produce energy.

Fall:

I recommend getting a glutathione infusion with B vitamins to boost your immune system during the time all the viruses and bacteria come out to play. Glutathione is your body's strongest antioxidant and helps your body to detoxify. B vitamins are also necessary for your immune cells to function properly.

Find my Winter & Spring recommendations in the next MM Publication.

Meet The Nurse:

As a registered nurse I err on the holistic side of medicine. I see the beauty and power of the body's ability to heal itself with the right nutrients. I help people get back to their roots and teach about vitamin and supplement alternatives that can restore health. I started my vitamin and hydration business to help people feel their best.

My company is called Wellness with Summer because I truly believe we all have the ability to feel the wellness our body desires. Come and see me in the Temecula valley for an IV infusion or a vitamin shot. I look forward to helping you feel your best.

Tia Esther Photography

SPECTRUMS OF COLOR

by Charis Gaston, LMFT

LEARN HOW COLORS AFFECT US ON AN EMOTIONAL, BIOLOGICAL, AND PSYCHOLOGICAL LEVEL.

WARM COLORS FOR SUMMER & FALL

RED...

I Feel...
Anger
Love
Passion
Alert
Desire
Excitement

I Think...
Danger
Strength
Power
Fire/Heat
Romance

My Body...
-Raises blood pressure
-Increases rate of respiration
-Stimulates adrenal glands
-Enhances metabolism

ORANGE...

I Feel...
Happiness
Confidence
Social
Overstimulated
Frustrated

I Think...
Warmth
Resourceful-ness
Draws
Attention

My Body...
-Increases sexuality
-Stimulates appetite
-Reduces fatigue
-Stimulates organ function

YELLOW...

I Feel...
Joy
Pleasure
Optimism
Cowardly

I Think...
Wisdom
Memorable
Hope
Wealth
Decay

My Body...
-Stimulates nervous system
-Stimulates memory & brain activity
-Promote mental clarity
-Release serotonin

Scan the QR Code to connect with Charis

FIND THE COOL COLORS IN THE NEXT MM PUBLICATION

DIY Sunscreen from Avid Oil Lady

"You know it's time to purge what isn't serving when life gives you feedback in the form of conflict, health challenges, or difficulty seeing things differently. I got into making most of my own household items and skincare products about 9 years ago when I was introduced to essential oils and natural solutions."

Ingredients

- 1/4 CUP BEESWAX (MAKES WATERPROOF)
- 2 TABLESPOONS SHEA BUTTER
- 1/4 CUP OF COCONUT OIL
- 1/2 CUP OLIVE OIL
- 2 TABLESPOONS OF ZINC POWDER
- 2 TEASPOONS OF VITAMIN E OIL
- ESSENTIAL OILS: 5 DROPS HELICHRYSUM, 5 DROPS PEPPERMINT, 5 DROPS LAVENDER

Method

1. Combine beeswax, shea butter, coconut oil and olive oil into a Mason jar or pot.
2. Stir over low heat until liquid runs clear. Remove from heat.
3. Add zinc, vitamin E oil and essential oils.
4. Stir and add to your choice of container to cool.
5. Use as needed!

My favorite DIY projects are cleaning products, candles, body scrubs, and natural sunscreen.
If you'd like to learn more about plant based natural solutions and how to use Essential oils, I'm your girl!

**PLEASE REMEMBER TO BE AWARE OF PHOTOSENSITIVITY WHEN USING CERTAIN OILS, SUCH AS CITRUS. SKIN CAN BE MORE SENSITIVE IN SUNLIGHT

Scan the QR Code to connect with Nicole

One of the #1 things our
customers love is feeling like
they belong...
And here, *you do*.

18

TIME SERVED IN WOMEN'S GROUPS

BY STORI NAGEL

Where two or more are gathered there's gonna be a problem. Especially if you don't conform, bodily or otherwise. The feeling that I was somehow very different became apparent in second grade, throughout highschool and right into adult life. I learned early on in the relationship, to stay close to my husband where it felt safe. I had a small friend group, but they were mainly pen pals. I learned church life was expected after marriage, it was not a negotiation. Religion always interested me, and I wanted to be a good wife, so I went along with it. When the children were all in school,

I began attending the 'Women's group.'

Women's group at church was a place where the women folk could speak freely. Before the study began, we crowded around a beautifully burnt Pyrex or organized holiday tea…. This is where the real 'tea' was spilled without recourse. _____

One day I remember being cornered between the portable buildings. "You know you should really try to be more modest. You are causing the men to stumble... We wouldn't want to cause someone else to sin...would we?" I compared what I wore most days, a tee shirt and jeans, with what everyone else wore...you guessed it - a tee shirt and jeans. So the deciding factor felt like it was my body.

I needed no encouragement to punish myself. Prayers at night consisted of pleads to make me something other than what I was, because what I was....was bad. I started out on The South Beach Diet. Dieting made everything else smaller but- jokes on you, my breasts stayed the same. *I was feeling healthier but not holier.*

I began to starve myself with little to no food and handfuls of vitamins. I got really sick. It felt like I was over medicated and tired, but sleep was never restful. The tests looked great, the illness was a mystery. It felt as if it was all in my head.

We switched churches, and I kept well away from any kind of 'fellowship'. I took Tai Chi, then Yoga to truly bring my life energy back up. About 8 years later, I found out I had adrenal fatigue. But I spent years perplexed as to what truly fueled the eating disorder. It was the result of woman-on-woman attacks, the competitive way western society divides women. The way they weaponized religion against me being different. The way playground bullies weaponized popularity.

In 2012 my breasts were lost to cancer, a casualty of their supposed threat to mankind. It was also then, through the isolation of treatment that I began to learn to love my body as it was, perfected in God's image, resilient and wonderful.

I developed an eating disorder, not wholly but in large part, because of how church socialization affected me as a curvy autistic woman. The 'not good enough' was not just from the platinum blonde, thin models all over mainstream media, but spiritually I was 'not good enough'. The self-flagellation I'd quietly done in small ways was amplified by their criticism. **To not look acceptable is one thing, but to be unholy... well that's a whole different kinda terrible.**

> "In 2012, my breasts were lost to cancer, a casualty of their supposed threat to mankind."

HAUS OF VOLTA
for survivors

FUNK N' FRESH FARM

I began my skin healing journey by exploring the benefits of goat milk. With a goat herd producing more milk than I could use on a daily basis, and a freezer full of homemade goat cheese, I started researching other ways to use goat milk. I have a skin disorder that causes my skin to be extremely dry, so lotion was the way to go. The more I learned about skincare formulation, the more I was hooked on the benefits of goat milk for skin.

In a few short months I began to see major changes in my skin. The first thing I noticed was the bumps on the back of my arms (known as keratosis pilaris) were disappearing! The skin on my hands and feet were actually starting to feel hydrated and soft for the first time in my life. I was on the way to healing my skin.

Healthy skin is a journey. Not only do we have to treat the outside, we have to treat the inside as well. Whatever is affecting you on the inside will show up on your skin. We can build rituals around self-care to ensure we stay on the path. Self-care includes nourishing our bodies with healthy foods, making time for meditation or other balancing activities, and following a skincare ritual tailored to our skin's needs.

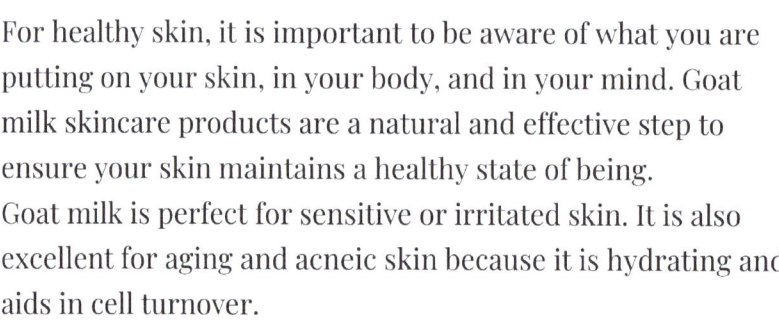

Visit Funk n Fresh Online

-Liz Funk, Founder

For healthy skin, it is important to be aware of what you are putting on your skin, in your body, and in your mind. Goat milk skincare products are a natural and effective step to ensure your skin maintains a healthy state of being.

Goat milk is perfect for sensitive or irritated skin. It is also excellent for aging and acneic skin because it is hydrating and aids in cell turnover.

Other benefits of goat milk include:

1. Soothes irritated, inflamed, tight, and itchy skin
2. Contains anti-inflammatory properties that will miraculously heal a sunburn overnight
3. Leaves your skin smoother and clearer due to a high concentration of Lactic Acid and a gentle alpha-hydroxy acid which has a light exfoliating effect
4. High in skin essential vitamins and lipids
5. Humectant properties attract water to the skin. When included in lotions we see a reduction of trans-epidermal water loss (water evaporation from your skin)

WHAT'S IN SEASON?

By Alicia Richardson

SUMMER	FALL	WINTER	SPRING
-avocado	-apples	-broccoli	-arugula
-bell peppers	-cauliflower	-brussels	-asparagus
-basil	-celery	sprouts	-chard & lettuce
-berries	-celery root	-cabbage	-cherries
-corn	-cranberry	-clementines	-dandelion greens
-cucumbers	-mushrooms	-meyer lemons	-fava beans
-figs	-persimmons	-oranges	-fennel
-grapes	-pomegranates	-pomelos	-garlic scapes
-green beans	-pumpkins	-tangerines	-kiwi
-melons	-pears	-winter	-kumquat
-zucchini	-sweet potatoes	squashes	-leeks
-tomatillos	-rutabagas		-nettles
-tomatoes	-potatoes		-parsley
-okra			-peas
-stone fruits			-radishes
			-rhubarb
			-spring onions
			-turnips

YEAR ROUND BONUS TIP:

Most of your herbs, collard greens, spinach, and root vegetables like potatoes, onions, beets and carrots are in season all year round!

Why Eat Seasonally?

1. Get more nourishment! Produce that is locally in season is more fresh & nutrient dense.
2. Reduce your carbon footprint. Shipping and large farming has a harmful effect on the environment.
3. Stay in alignment with Mother Earth and the Wheel of the Year.
4. Save money. Typically markets offer sales on food that is in season.

Scan the QR Code to Connect with Alicia

WHEEL OF THE YEAR
WORD SEARCH

By Pamela Buehl

```
Z L M Y B J O S J B P I I N M X O K F A
D Z C J B R B I O V I M B O L C S R Z K
X T P E A R T H G U L T L A J E T E S L
G Y I D D H Q J Z S L S T K J C A B D G
T O W A L P U R G I S Z R W M P R I M V
M O R G F G X C D N Y W N L W B A R K C
S D G N S S M M I N D D F Y I H C T H S
J W I N T E R S O L S T I C E T F H Q T
Y W K C Y U K P S D E N E H P H H X D O
O Q R V M T D I S T W J E R Y Z I A G D
H H R I L V D E A T H F S A M H A I N K
W A T E R J S U M M E R S O L S T I C E
K R I H X Z W W A N B R D N M D A K D R
H R P H E T R C A N D E L T M A S K X T
Z R B E L T A N E S M B M D R B Y H N Q
R U F F U I E E U R O T S M R K H E M O
T I F L I H F I R D O A C N A M Q R A S
L N A D L A M M A S A K I K K D G I B O
H Y U L E Z V B O D Y D C R I J C F O G
J I M F P S L L U G H N A S S A D T N S
```

SUMMER SOLSTICE
OSTARA
REBIRTH
WATER
MIND
WALPURGIS
IMBOLC
EARTH
DEATH
MABON
LUGHNASSAD
BELTANE
SAMHAIN
BODY
LITHA
LAMMAS
SOUL
LIFE
YULE
AIR
WINTER SOLSTICE

'IT'S OKAY TO READ ROMANCE'

an Unexpected Journey to Self-Discovery

by Tracy Herzog, M.S.

It was late summer in 2015 and I had just returned to work after the birth of my first child. The sun was shining, the a/c cranked to full-blast, and I was listening to book reviews on NPR. I was also neck-deep in an intense phase of life transition that would take years to fully grasp and work through. But on that day, I was trucking along, blindly endeavoring to maintain my professional identity while navigating my role as a mother.

It was to the soundtrack of literary discourse that I traversed the route home. I had those good vibes moms get when they are in the car alone and not having to worry about a fussing baby, passing snacks to the back seat, or anyone falling asleep before their usual nap time, thus causing a cascade of timing issues that would take the remainder of the day to recover from. I was flying blissfully solo and feeling as if I were my former self, the now-elusive individual version of me.

I was only half-present, my focus split between the sun, the road, and book reviews, when there came a preface which caught my attention. I can't recall it verbatim, but rest assured it went something like this: "We are going to talk about romance novels; Reputable public radio listeners, please do not change the station."

I reached for the dial. I very likely rolled my eyes in distaste at the very thought of squandering my precious time on grocery store bodice rippers. That stuff was trash, wasn't it?

Completely unbeknownst to me, my literary tastes were stuck up, bougie, and dated. Only the likes of Steinbeck, Orwell, Kerouac, Bukowski, Vonnegut, Fitzgerald, and Salinger graced my bookshelves and the nearest I'd allow myself to a romance novel was Austen, who I stringently viewed through the lens of classic literature and not smutty romance. In other words, I was so tangled in the patriarchal web I didn't even know where I was.

I would like to take a moment to point out the salience of NPR's preemptive warning. Women's literature is inexplicably devalued by our society to the point that we must preface it before we can discuss it. Romance, in particular, receives the brunt of the prejudice. Interestingly, romance as a literary genre is by women and for women. At every stage in this process, women are at the helm—serving as the authors, editors, publishers, cover artists, and consumers. Let's say this loud and proud people: Romance is a feminist genre. Not only that, but romance is the highest grossing genre by a landslide, generating 1.4 billion dollars annually (Curcic, 2022). You would need to combine both the second (crime/mystery) and third (religious/inspirational) grossing genres to be able to hold a candle to romance.

With numbers like that, how can it be viewed as a low-brow, frivolous, and illegitimate child of literature and not the powerhouse that it is?

continued

That's a big question that cannot be resolved in the scope of this article alone. Suffice to say the answer lies somewhere in the way our culture values women's work, sexuality, and how deserving they are of pleasure.

Driving home that day, I was granted permission by the NPR Gods to give romance a chance. I cooked dinner for my family, put the baby to bed, and as she co-slept beside me I scanned my Kindle for possible reads. Still skeptical, I probably spent about an hour perusing options —and there are a lot of options depending on one's tastes. When I finally settled on a novel, I didn't put it down again until it was finished.

Sleep deprived and stumbling into the break room the next day, I announced, "I read my first romance novel last night."

My boss asked what I thought.

"I think I'm in trouble."

Thus began a book a day craving. This was my escape, my inner world, my joy—a place where I felt safe, free from the pressures of my relational roles. I joined Facebook groups for the subgenres I loved most and was met by profoundly welcoming women who spoke often and openly about sexuality, desire, trauma, managing emotional safety, and...absolutely wild sexual interests. I'm talking demons, scales, shifters, prehensile tails, dinosaur love, bird-men, tentacles, you name it—romance has got you covered. These days, we aren't limited to Fabio on a pirate ship. That being said, if you are into Fabio on a pirate ship, he is indeed available. Choice is the theme, and each reader's ability to claim what they want down to the most creative nuance.

continued

TIA ESTHER PHOTOGRAPHY

Arguments have been floating around since the 1970's that romance is in actuality a misogynistic genre encouraging women to "cherish the chains of their bondage" (The Female Eunuch; Greer 281). I can't speak to the romance novels of the 1970s, but I'm happy to talk about tropes. There are lots of storylines available. Some do feature muscled, alpha, heroes to whom the heroine falls madly in love with—that is a single stylistic trope among many. But I propose that if one does choose to read about a male/female romantic dyad, it isn't by definition misogynistic so much as it is simply heterosexual. What most readers are attracted to is the lack of subjugation, the innate power, and undeniable value each relatable heroine possesses. Not to mention the sexual gratification she receives. How could that not be attractive? We live in a world where women are taught to serve, to get by on less, to draw constantly from the well of our hearts and to never have it refilled in return. The romance novel is a place where women are given the same level of care that they give. It is a safe place to explore and discover our sexuality, when our own bedrooms and partners do not always offer such unconditional protection. I counter that the romance novel is not a mode of oppression, but a gateway to sexual liberation.

I don't just read romance novels anymore. I write them. But there was a time in my life, on a sunny drive home from work, when I needed permission to explore certain avenues of my identity—the feminine side, the sexual self, the adventurer within. This genre led me on an unexpected journey of self-discovery, one that ultimately altered my entire career path. And while not everyone will experience such a foundational shift when picking up one of those deliciously smutty, grocery store, bodice rippers—romance might still take you somewhere unexpected. Perhaps you're like me and you need permission to crack a racy cover. Or you could be looking for someone to tell you that it's okay to enjoy women's literature or to even talk about it. If so, here you go: It's more than okay. Reading stories about women's happiness and pleasure is neither frivolous nor low brow—it's freeing. More than that, it's radical feminism.

Sources

Curcic, Dimitrije. "Romance Novel Sales Statistics." Wordsrated, October, 9th 2022, https://wordsrated.com/romance-novel-sales-statistics/.

Greer, Germaine. The Female Eunuch. MacGibbon and Kee, 1970.

> **"Romance, as a literary genre, is by women and for women."**
> -*Tracy Herzog, M.S.*

SCAN THE QR CODE TO CONNECT WITH TRACY

SUPPORTING YOUR OWN HEALING JOURNEY

BY DEDE JONES

1. Find Community.
We are all on the same journey, it just looks a bit different for everyone.

2. Listen to your body.
Tune into symptoms as cues and get to the root cause. Incorporate movement everyday.

3. Align with the seasons.
Follow the Wheel of the Year and Ayurvedic Scheduling for more efficient time management.

4. Don't stop.
We are always going to be on the journey. There is no 'all healed and perfect'

BOOK RECOMMENDATIONS:

- *A Mind of Your Own by Kelly Brogan*
- *Witch by Lisa Lister*
- *Herbal Healing for Women by Rosemary Gladstar*
- *Journey Back to Health by Sharissa Bradley*

SCAN THE QR CODE TO CONNECT WITH DEDE ON INSTAGRAM

Make Your Own Kombucha

"I love making and drinking kombucha! It's so fun and ridiculously easy to make. It's an ancient tradition, originating in Asia 220 B.C.. It has so many healing benefits. Ditch your probiotic and add daily fermented foods. It is so much cheaper and more effective." -Christina

Kombucha & Pregnancy: Keep your gut healthy and reduce the incidence of hosting GBS by incorporating fermented foods. Kombucha is safe to ferment and consume in pregnancy. Any of my clients that want to brew their own kombucha leave with a SCOBY! It's so fun to hear of their stories of kombucha making.

Supplies Needed:

- Temperature sticker for jar
- 1 gallon jar with my Muslim fabric lid and rubber band
- 1 quart sized Mason jar
- 1 SCOBY with two cups of starter fluid (you can order online or ask a friend or grow your own)
- 8 organic black tea bags
- 1 cup of sugar

with Christina Sanders, LM, CPM

KOMBUCHA RECIPE

1. Rinse all your stuff! Don't use much soap, if any. Add circle sticker and temperature sticker to the 1 gallon jar.
2. Bring to boil 4-5 cups of water.
3. Pour 8 cups of water into 1 gallon container.
4. Place 8 tea bags in the 1 qt. glass mason jar, pour water from tea pot and let steep for 15 minutes
5. After 15 minutes take the tea bags out and pour in 1 cup of sugar and stir to dissolve. Then pour contents into 1 gallon jar (that already has 8 cups of water in it)
6. Let that sit until the temp gauge shows the 86 temp range. You don't want it too hot, it would kill the bacteria in the SCOBY.
7. When it's 86 degrees fahrenheit or below put the SCOBY and starter fluid (the fluid in the bag with the SCOBY) in the 1 gallon jar.
8. Place the cloth and rubber band to cover it. Make sure the sticker is on the 1 gallon jar and place the date. To keep track of brewing times. This helps to adjust next batch if needed based on your sticker history of how long you did batches.
9. Put in a darkish cupboard and don't even check it for one week.
10. I would guess it will take a full two weeks for your first brew. All I am checking for is if it's too sweet. That means not enough fermentation has occurred. It hasn't eaten the sugar. I also am making sure the baby SCOBY that starts to form is decently thick. Once those two things feel right you can drink it or do a second ferment.

SCAN THE QR CODE TO CONNECT WITH CHRISTINA THE MIDWIFE

FINDING SAFETY IN EXPRESSION

We deserve to feel safe expressing ourselves authentically and creatively.

Meditation Sessions, Salsa Basics and Yoga Wellness

SCAN THE QR CODE TO CONNECT
WITH ROXANNE ON INSTAGRAM

Images by Tia Esther Photography

Roxanne's Journey

Roxanne grew up loving dance. However, there were several years that she hid it from herself and others. She thought she wasn't good enough, afraid to "make any sudden moves". She found it difficult to express herself verbally, emotionally, and especially creatively. She thought, "I'm not an artist or a dancer, I don't have talent like other people."

Thankfully that began to change as she embarked on a personal and spiritual path in 2008. She moved to Hawaii where she started learning yoga and teaching salsa basics. In 2010, she got certified to teach Zumba but still didn't feel quite ready, yet. She then traveled Central and South America, backpacking with a partner for over a year. After this, she spent a year living in Mexico and 6 months teaching English. *These experiences helped her connect with the land*, and natural spiritual practices of Latin culture. Each step along the way, she encouraged herself to open up, to not be so shy, but it wasn't easy. Through classes in shadow work, attunement, yoga and wellness training, Roxanne has developed a unique method for nurturing Self into the next step.

Her Meditations by Design are created uniquely for her clients situational growth. First by gently identifying current feelings and needs, then working with the elements of nature and the intrinsic healing power of the body, while creating harmony between heart and mind. She brings this same feeling of safety into her dance and yoga classes. Roxanne believes we should all feel safe in our body. She's excited to share these tools with others so they can feel the joy and freedom of being their authentic Self.

Lowering Food Waste
One Leftover at a Time

BY JESSE ST JAMES

Photo: Alicia Richardson | Tia Esther

My favorite way to reinvent (and hide some veggies from my family) is to make potato soup or tomato sauce. I blend up my old veggies and incorporate them into either the soup or sauce. Any of these vegetables could be repurposed: broccoli, carrots, cauliflower, brussel sprouts, green beans, tomatoes, you name it.

The estimated amount of food waste in the US ranges between 35-103 million tons per year. To put that into perspective, *30-40% of household food goes uneaten.* The equivalent to 20 pounds per person per month. That means Americans are throwing out approximately $165 billion in food each year! If your social media timeline is as 'crunchy' as mine you've seen many online tips and tricks and an endless amount of information on waste. It can become overwhelming. Here are some ways to turn our attention to food waste in our own homes.

For leftover meat, the crock pot comes to the rescue. Many times I've experienced disappointments when trying out new recipes that didn't quite turn out the way I was hoping. I couldn't bring myself to throw the results away. I taught myself to use my handy dandy crock pot to reinvent my little dinner mistakes. For example, I once made a pork shoulder in the oven and it came out tough and unappetizing. I could not bring myself to throw away pounds of meat. I tested putting the tough meat into the crock pot with a bottle of BBQ sauce and made pulled pork sliders for dinner. This is just one example of remaking a "meal gone wrong" but the same formula can be applied to almost any leftover.

Congee: a Leftover Go-To

- Leftover rice, veggies & meat
- Minced ginger
- Chili oil
- Sesame oil
- Bone broth or stock
- Soy sauce or coconut aminos
- A blender or food processor

- Start with any leftover protein or fresh cooked protein, if you prefer. Chicken gets put into the crockpot early in the day so it's nice and tender by dinner time.
- Take between 2-4 cups of leftover rice and add double the amount of broth/stock to a pot. Let it cook on medium heat for 5-10 mins.
- In a separate pan, sauté leftover vegetables in sesame oil with chopped garlic (garlic powder works too) and any other seasonings you'd like.
- After the rice has started to break down in the broth and the vegetables are soft and fragrant, take a cup of broth from the pot along with the vegetables, and blend in a blender.
- Pour the blended mixture into the broth and rice along with 1-2 tablespoons of minced ginger, 1-4 tablespoons of chili oil (depending on your preferred spice level), and 1-4 teaspoons of soy sauce, and sesame oil and let that simmer on low for about 10-15 minutes.
- Take the entire pot and blend it to the desired consistency. Shred the chicken and add it into the pot.
- Pour the warm congee into big bowls and top with more sesame and chili oil.
- Enjoy!

A Simple Guide to
INTUITIVE TAROT

WITH VIVIANNA SEVERANCE

Quality over quantity

Less is more when it comes to pulling cards. Begin by pulling only one card and allow your gaze to soften as you view the card and process all the information available in the symbolism and artwork. Notice, what was the first thing you saw in the card? What is its significance to you at this moment? How did the image or wording of the card make you feel?

Put The Book Down

As tempting as it is to seek information outside of ourselves, don't let this be your first step. Everything we need to know is already within us. Always begin reading your card by first noticing the thoughts, feelings, or ideas that come. Take a moment to journal your initial impressions. THEN feel free to add to your notes from available books or online sources.

Experience

Allow the cards to tell you a story. Immerse yourself and imagine what it would feel like to enter the scene. What are the figures doing or saying? How does this relate to your question or situation?

Just Let Go

Tarot is a tool that helps strengthen your intuition. Being in your head about what each card "means" can disconnect you. Let go of expectations, fear, or worry that you have made a mistake. There are no mistakes in Tarot!

Community

Find like minded friends to practice with. Create your own Tarot Circles. Tarot began as a game when it was created, so remember to play!

31

What If You Were...
A TAROT CARD
An Explorative Art Meditation

Tarot cards have been described as individual pieces of art. The feeling of the imagery begins in the body. When viewing a painting in a museum, we begin developing our own understanding of what the artist intended.

Some will come away with a similar impression, while others may have a different interpretation of what the artist wanted us to see and feel. The best artists leave the translation up to the viewer. This same beautiful approach can be taken with reading Tarot. Your understanding will be specific to your experience and situation.

What if your life, your situation, or your worries was a Tarot card? What would it feel like? What would it look like? I invite you to take a step outside of the box, by creating a card based on you. Use any artistic medium you have available to you. Such as pencils, pens, paint, or markers.

Vivianna is a certified MM Facilitator, yoga teacher, reiki master, intuitive oracle & tarot guide & AromaTouch therapist. She gathers women for healing and reconnection.

SCAN THE
QR CODE
TO CONNECT
WITH VIVIANNA AT THE
RAVEN'S NEST

1. Begin by taking time to pause, use your breath ease into your body. Allow thoughts to pass by like cars on a speeding freeway, always coming back to your breath.
2. Imagine a Tarot scene and begin to take note of the time of day. Is the sun out, the moon? Cloudy, stormy, raining, or clear?
3. What does the landscape look and feel like? Is it dry, wet, cold? Are there any natural elements in this card that stand out to you?
4. Are you the figure in the card, or is there a different version of you?
5. Perhaps there is someone else there. Take note of details. If you have one, what is the figure doing?
6. Do you sense or see any animals? What are they doing?
7. Do you see any symbols or meaningful items?
8. If you were a suit, which would you be?
   - Earth – Pentacles
   - Air – Swords
   - Fire – Wands
   - Water – Cups
9. What colors stand out on your card?

Allow your card to develop without judgment, or stress about how it looks as it is coming together. This is an exercise in trusting yourself. Perhaps you will give yourself exactly what you need to know or see right now.

Submit your personal Tarot Card for a chance to be featured in a future publication!
Send Submissions To:
kristen@mermaidmovement.online

ASTROLOGY FORECAST

GEMINI

The High Priestess, 10 of Wands, The Empress

You've been focused on yourself and it's paying off, this focus has kept you distanced from others and you're very much in the cerebral realm. You've been working hard on a creative project and it feels burdensome at times, but keep going, you're so close to the finish line and the end of this chapter will take you from your High Priestess energy into your Empress energy, get ready to flourish in the coming months and embrace the queen energy you were made to embody.

LEO

The World, The Wheel of Fortune, 9 of Wands

The World is literally at your fingertips, and it has been for a while. You're on the precipice of something great but there is something holding you back. Fear of the unknown perhaps? Take the leap of faith and trust that the Wheel of Fortune will turn in your favor. Be open to a little chaos and new challenges as they arise on your journey. Whatever this new adventure is, keep it to yourself at first. It may be tempting to shout it from the rooftops, but too many outside influences and opinions may muddy the waters in the beginning stages of this endeavor.

LIBRA

Knight of Pentacles, Ace of Pentacles, The Magician

There is no shortage of abundance in your life. You've worked hard building your home and a strong community around you. Your resources are a powerful catalyst for whatever is coming next. No matter which path you take, you have everything you need and more to create something truly magical.

CANCER

King of Cups, 8 of Swords, 8 of Pentacles

You are the master of your emotions, trust the process and try not to get too in your head. Leaning into your powerful intuition will serve you well. When things feel overwhelming in the coming months, focus on your work and your environment. Creating a stable and balanced foundation is the key to success for you.

VIRGO

2 of Cups, Page of Cups, The Sun

You've been learning how to get out of your head and listen to your heart, this is a big change for you! New connections and communities have helped with this internal shift. Continue down the path that you're on and continue to nurture these connections and relationships, only more good will come of it. The Sun card says that your future couldn't be brighter!

SCORPIO

The Fool, The High Priestess, 3 of Pentacles

You are endlessly curious and have a passion for life and new discoveries. You know yourself well and have a strong moral compass and a sense of balance, you are fiercely independent which has served you well thus far. Perhaps, in the coming months, it's time to expand and soften, collaborate with others in different industries and with different perspectives to help you continue your growth.

Tune in further with Moira Jamey Flora

SEE PART TWO IN THE NEXT PUBLICATION

TIA ESTHER PHOTOGRAPHY

Pivotal Moments

Trusting A Mother's Intuition
By Adriane Alvarez

DAY ONE:

Around 8:30 pm I noticed more fluids, and I texted my doula, "If my water broke I would know right lol?" We went over early labor one more time and I began to notice some cramping around 10 pm. The plan was to sleep as much as I could through early labor, so I did.

DAY TWO:
MORNING...

The contractions picked up in intensity around sunrise. I checked in with my birth team and labored through the morning with my husband, Joe. Right before noon, my midwife came to my house and she checked me. She said I was 2 cm dilated, and suggested Spinning Babies techniques to help get the baby into position.

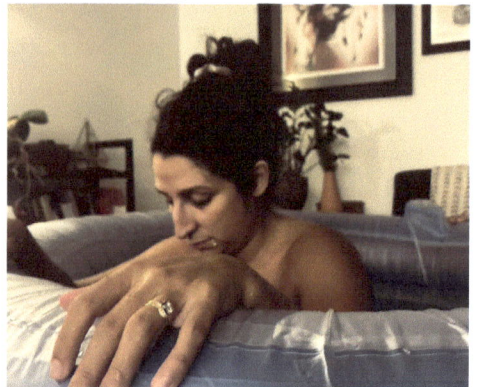

AFTERNOON-

The midwife left and we worked through contractions in different positions for the next few hours. I floated in the pool and was stung by a bee. I texted my doula at 4:15 pm- "Just threw up all my smoothie. It was awful coming up." She knew this was a sign that things were progressing so she made her way over.

EVENING-

As the sun was setting, contractions were intensifying and getting closer together. We called the midwives back, and my husband began to fill the birth tub as my doula worked with me through contractions. I got into the tub shortly before the midwives arrived. This is where the story took a slight shift...

UPON ARRIVAL...

the midwives did a quick assessment and recommended getting out of the tub. We decided the water was a little too warm and was causing the baby's heart rate to increase slightly. Once I was out of the tub, everyone's vitals were stable but my contractions were slowing. My midwives began to suggest that I transfer to the hospital due to 'failure to progress' but I knew I was not ready to give in. I still had so much more to give. This was a PIVOTAL MOMENT.

I remember asking "What happens if I don't transfer to the hospital per your recommendation?" And the midwife, visibly frustrated, said "Well, I don't know. No one has ever done that." This made me feel like my midwives were questioning me, or that I was making an unsafe decision. The support from my husband and my doula kept me going, kept me trusting my intuition. Around 11:15 pm, we all decided to try for a little rest and I laid in bed with my husband.

DAY THREE: MORNING

Around 2 am, the midwives and doula decided to leave and let me rest. I was able to sleep in between contractions and rejuvenate my body a bit.

I woke up feeling a little defeated, my contractions were slower and less intense than before. I lost trust in my midwives. My doula came back around 7 am to help me reset, and the next shift was underway.

Joe suggested that I call another midwife that had been supporting me through my pregnancy. She taught my childbirth education classes and provided my prenatal massages and bodywork. I loved her. She would know what to do. She had all of the right things to say, and I regained my power and my mindset. I had the strength to keep going...

AFTERNOON...

I spent the day in the summer sun, floating in my pool and resting. I even got stung by a bee at one point! That has to be rare during labor, right? I showered and snuggled Joe and did more Spinning Babies until around 3 pm when my contractions started coming on back to back. They were stronger. My doula came back again around 3:30 pm, and I decided I did not want to call my original midwives back to my birth space.

EVENING...

I called my trusted midwife back, and she came to be by my side. This was a PIVOTAL MOMENT. She arrived at 6:30 pm and her presence made me feel safe to keep going. I just knew that she was the right midwife for me. She suggested so many different positions and techniques to help bring my baby down, and physically supported me through each one of them. We did this all through the night until 11:30 pm when it was time to refill the tub.

DAY FOUR:

At 12:08 am I got back in the tub. A second midwife arrived shortly after to support my trusted midwife. A little over an hour later, I felt the urge to push. I remember these contractions being the most intense part, even more than the actual birth. I pushed with contractions for an hour and a half in the tub, and around 3:45 am the midwives suggested that I get back onto land to push the baby out.

I pushed so hard all of the blood capillaries in my eyes burst. I knew I was not going to give up. I never thought that was even an option. With every contraction I grabbed my doula's hands and curled around my baby, bringing her down with every push. At 5:28 am, my baby was born and I pulled her up onto my chest. I instinctively cleared her nose and airways with my mouth and breathed her in. She was here. I did it.

SCAN THE QR CODE TO FIND YOGA CLASSES WITH ADRIANE

ADRIANE'S 3 TIPS FOR STRENGTH DURING LABOR:
1 - Consistent yoga practice before and during pregnancy
2 - Testing endurance in all life situations
3 - Daily outdoor walks throughout pregnancy

HOME

A BODY MIND SOUL YOGA STUDIO

In Person Classes
Community
Workshops
Teacher Trainings
Holistic Healing Services

FIRST MONTH OF
UNLIMITED MEMBERSHIP
FOR $49

DISCOVER
THE TRANSFORMATIVE POWER OF YOGA

SIGN UP TODAY

Homeyogatemecula.com
@homeyogatemecula

A MOVEMENT MEDITATION
FOR WOMEN'S HEALTH BY ASHLEY LLANO

This opening meditation and breath work is great for **grounding**, and the seated movement is great for *warming* and creating **fluidity** in the pelvis and all of the supporting muscles. This practice also has downward movement of energy, so this is a great tool to facilitate *release*. Think along the lines of detoxification, or for women who are on their moon cycle. Helping to keep the energy flowing down, so that the inhale and breath can be used for bringing in Love, Compassion and Kindness.

We begin by stilling the mind. Start by having a seat. This can be in the form of sitting on a cushion, leaning back against a chair, or sitting on the floor leaning against a couch.
Whichever position you choose it is important to feel supported and comfortable.

Close your eyes. Let go of any idea of controlling the breath. Let the breath "be". With each exhale let your attention and focus move down, down to the floor beneath you. Feel all the parts of your body that are touching the floor, feel the temperature, the texture. Ask yourself, is the floor hard, or soft like carpet, or a yoga mat?

Place one hand on your belly and one hand on your chest. Begin to take notice of your breath. Take notice of the movement of your body, as you inhale and exhale. Can you feel the rise and fall of your belly or your chest?
On the next inhale, breathe all the way down to your belly. Try to breathe your bellybutton into your hand, as you exhale, notice the belly moving back down and in towards the spine. Do this for 5 whole breaths.

On the next exhale use your abdominals to push the breath out, while keeping a light engagement of your belly, as you inhale moving your breath up into the hand that is over your heart.
Visualize the inflation of the lungs, the expansion of the ribcage, the lift and lengthening of your spine. Now notice that when you inhale you lift up and lengthen the front of the body and on the exhale you soften down the back of the body.

While in a crossed legged seated position use your breath to move your body. On every inhale press the chest forward into Cat position and every exhale fold the body over for Cow position.
Practice this for 5 full breaths.
Continue by placing your left hand on the floor next to your left hip, inhale the right arm up by the ear and lean to the left side. Walk the hands forward into a forward fold.

Switch the cross of the legs, so the top leg moves to the bottom. In this position inhale the body forward to Cat position and exhale to Cow position.
Then, place your right hand on the floor next to your right hip, inhale the left arm up, by the ear and lean to the right. Walk the hands forward into a forward fold over the legs. Notice the difference from one side to the other.

WHAT A SOUND BATH DOES TO YOUR BRAIN

by Vivianna Severance

A sound bath can consist of singing bowls made of different kinds of metal and crystal, as well as gongs, tuning forks, and chimes. It is usually experienced by laying on the floor on a comfortable mat with pillows, bolsters, and blankets to keep you comfortable throughout the experience.

A sound bath creates a meditative state where the brain emits healing brainwaves. Different tones and frequencies help reduce stress and anxiety.

When we spend too much time in Gamma and Beta, the brain sends signals to produce cortisol which can be damaging to the body. During a sound bath, the brain can shift from the beta state to alpha and theta states, which can promote a sense of calm and well-being. By reducing stress, tension, and anxiety, the body begins to repair itself. The vibrations and sounds can create a sense of physical and mental release, allowing for deep relaxation and meditation. With sound baths widely available, this is a great first step into healing your brain and body by creating an environment conducive to growth vs. survival.

5 BRAIN WAVE FREQUENCIES

There are five brain wave frequencies, each correlating with a specific state of consciousness

1. *Gamma* - Awake, Processing
2. *Beta* - Alert, Decision Making
3. *Alpha* - Relaxed, Healing
4. *Theta* - Sleep, Deep Meditation
5. *Delta* - Deep Sleep, Unconscious

SOUND BATHS

MORE INSIGHTS FROM CLAIRE SCHEMBRI

Sound has the powerful ability to stir up mental habits and impressions that we're not aware of. In yoga, this phenomenon is called *samskaras*. Through the use of sound, impressions are stirred up and brought to the surface to be confronted. One popular sound modality is a sound bath. These can be an incredibly peaceful experience, but they can also be quite disruptive. This is a natural occurrence. Immersing yourself in a sound bath can cleanse the mind faster when compared to traditional meditation techniques. If you remain open and unattached, it can be a profound and transformative experience.

If you find it difficult to meditate, incorporating sound into your practice can be beneficial. *Humming*, *sighing*, *laughing*, and *singing* can all stimulate the vagus nerve, which helps to reduce stress, improve focus, and restore balance.

Sound is all around us, and it can be harnessed to improve our well-being. From the subtle pulsations of our bodies to the vast expanse of the universe, sound has the power to heal and transform.

Sound Healing

by Claire

PREGNANCY

"IT TAKES A VILLAGE TO RAISE A CHILD. IT TAKES A VILLAGE TO HOLD A MAMA."

Birth is a Pivotal Moment, a sacred passage that needs to be protected and celebrated. Postpartum, in reality, is an indefinite period of time. And motherhood is a forever evolving phase that has one Beginning and no End.

A Birth Team is a group of people who make you feel loved, empowered, and safe. Your birth team can include people such as your partner, doula, midwife, family and/or friends. It also can include a postpartum team- such as a postpartum doula or lactation consultant.

How to Build your Birth Village:

- Rally support to pay for the birth team. Put a doula fund on your registry.
- Have many open & genuine conversations with your partner to communicate how you want to feel while laboring, and how they could effectively support you.
- Set Boundaries. Avoid extra anxiety-inducing advice and extra noise. No advice from well meaning friends and family is the best advice.
- Follow Your Mama Intuition. Be well informed in order to make the best decision that will fit you and your baby
- Take a local childbirth class (outside of the hospital setting) to meet other moms and birth professionals.

–ISABEL CUEVAS

"BRIDGING THE GAP"
A BIRTH STORY OF TRUST & INTUITION
BY MEGAN MASLER

"Years before you were born, we met in that plane of existence between life and dreams. There was an instant pull towards one another that was so natural I never had any doubts that you were the soul that would one day be my baby. In this space there were no rules, just feelings and intuition. Eventually you decided it was finally time to come into existence. When I shared your presence with other people they would ask me if I was excited to meet you, but I already knew you."

Intuition led me to my baby and I continued to listen. Modern society and my education as a doula, lactation consultant, and RN told me that doctors and science know best. Genetic testing can tell us if your baby has any genetic diseases, ultrasounds show us that your baby is physically developing properly, and monthly check ups ensure that our babies are healthy...right? After all, how could it be possible to simply trust your body and baby? All of these ideas had been ground into me, but when I finally sat and listened to my body and my baby I realized that none of this was our path. For thousands of years the human race continued to exist before modern medicine and birth lay solely in the hands of women. And so I walked away from everything that I had been taught and my journey into motherhood began.

CONTINUED →

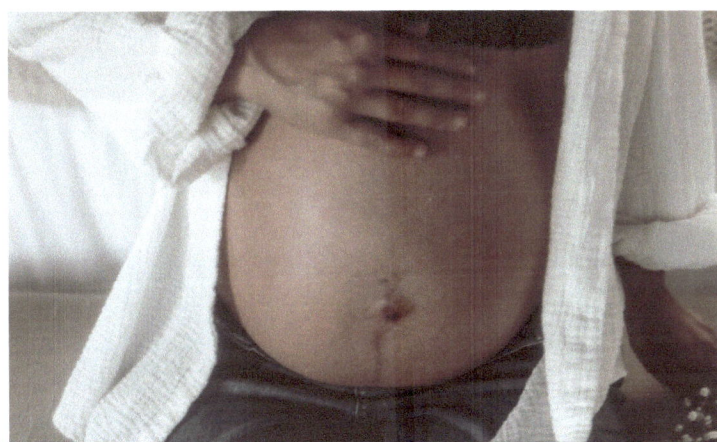

FIVE THINGS YOU PROBABLY DON'T KNOW ABOUT PREGNANCY AND POSTPARTUM:

1. You can keep your placenta. You deserve to see it, get to know it, and maybe even thank it!
2. You can learn about your baby's position and hear the heartbeat in your own home throughout pregnancy.
3. Postpartum is actually a sacred window, specifically set aside for healing and learning your baby - not "bouncing back".
4. There are specific herbs available to you that help with: preconception, breastfeeding, anxiety, blood building, milk production and more.
5. You can birth your baby by yourself.

-ALISHA MEYER,
TRADITIONAL BIRTH ATTENDANT

BRIDGING THE GAP

A BIRTH STORY OF TRUST & INTUITION BY MEGAN MASLER

CONTINUED FROM PAGE 42

I began to take charge of my pregnancy just as I have done in every other aspect of my life thus far. Mornings started with internal reflection and meditation to connect with my baby. Then came nourishing foods to assist my body in growing a healthy baby. In the afternoons I would take a break from work to rest and be with my baby. Evenings were filled with more nourishing foods and time spent with family and friends. As my belly grew, I learned how to belly map and find the position of my baby. If it felt right, I would listen to her heart beating strongly, reminding me that she was growing so perfectly. Every once in a while I would take my vital signs to ensure that my own body was functioning well, but most of all I listened and leaned into my intuition.

Nearly halfway through my pregnancy, I decided I wanted a little more support and hired a birth doula. She became a sounding board for my thoughts and feelings and patiently guided me back to my own intuition. I also decided to begin some chiropractic care and he taught me how to feel my belly for my baby and also encouraged me to turn inwards when I had any doubts. My husband fully trusted me in my intuition and ancestral knowledge.

On a Friday afternoon just before 40 weeks my baby decided it was time. I had fully expected to wait as long as she needed and was surprised when I started to feel signs of change. Contractions began slowly and continued for two nights and two days. We danced our labor dance, moving from the birth ball, to the bed, to the shower, and back to the bed. I fully trusted that my baby would tell me how she was doing. My doula assisted me in listening to my baby's heartbeat whenever I asked and my husband kept me hydrated and well fed.

I continued to check in with my baby and let her lead me. On the second night, I was pulled back to that in-between world. The veil between reality and dreamland was thinning and I felt that I would meet my baby soon. My baby had other plans.

The sun rose on that second full day of contractions and I started to falter. I began to think about whether this was progressing normally. Whether it was intuition on her part or the kind of knowledge that comes with experience, my doula asked me how I was feeling. In that moment, I was not sure, for you see, I had had premonitions and dreams of my baby's birth for months now. I never dreamed of having her at home; my visions always were of my baby wrapped in a hospital blanket with a little hat on her head. When my doula asked me how I was feeling, I already knew that my path was not to birth at home. I was terrified.

I had worked so hard, my entire pregnancy to maintain control over my body and my baby and I was so scared that I would be relinquishing this freedom by walking through those hospital doors. What I was met with surprised me. Respect and awe for my tenacity greeted me. The on-call OB met with me and asked what my birth plan was. I told her that I wanted to be asked before anything happened. I wanted minimal interventions and I would like to be the one to call the shots. The OB asked if I would like for my husband to be the one to catch the baby. She spent time creating a doll out of blankets and teaching him how to catch our baby.

After days of no sleep, I was exhausted, and really just wanted to check out. All I wanted to do was sleep, but my baby made sure that I paid attention to her and listened to my intuition. Contrary to my initial plan, I wound up asking for more assistance than I thought I would. Fortunately, I knew my rights, my body, and my baby, and I was able to advocate for myself and maintain agency over my own body. It was so empowering to have nurses and doctors ask me before they touched me, seek permission to share ideas with me, and truly trust that my body will do what it needs to.

After 75 hours of labor, I finally reached the end of the birth portal. I reached my hands through the veil, found my baby, and guided her earthside. The moment she touched my chest I knew this was her, the baby I had met so long ago. We looked at one another slowly and she rested quietly until she found her voice.

Nothing about this birth experience went as I thought it would. I never would have guessed that I would have asked for an epidural, for someone to release my waters, or have my labor augmented. What I did know deep down from very early on in pregnancy was that my baby was going to need assistance. I remember having conversations with my doula in my second trimester if she knew how to guide me through shoulder dystocia, hemorrhage, and neonatal resuscitation. Fortunately, I did not dismiss my intuition and was in a place of assistance when these things occurred.

My postpartum recovery was rough. A second degree tear and a hematoma prevented me from being able to move around easily and care for myself. This meant that I truly had to practice the rest that I teach new mothers in my practice as a postpartum doula and lactation consultant. Taking a page out of my own book, I had arranged to surround myself with women who could care for me in those first few weeks. I was brought meals, my house was cleaned, and our laundry done all while I snuggled my newborn in bed. Despite how uncomfortable I was physically, I was so well supported.

NORA

A Traditional Midwifery Secret for Women's Health

Herbal remedies have been used to nourish and heal people across all cultures for all recorded time. There are many different herbs and uses, but a great place to start for overall women's wellness is a cup of Nora tea.

Nora is a blend of four powerful herbs- Nettle leaf, Oatstraw, Red Raspberry leaf and Alfalfa- all of which have great benefits.

You can put 2-3 teaspoons of loose herb in a tea bag or steeper and drink a cup of Nora or try an *herbal infusion*.

Place a cup (by volume) of dried NORA herb in a quart jar and fill it to the top with boiling water. Tightly lid the jar and allow it to steep for 4-10 hours. After steeping, strain the plant material out, add honey, and drink the infusion. Drink the quart of infusion within 36 hours to avoid spoilage! Forgot to drink it in time? Share it with your plants! They'll love it, too.

SCAN THE QR CODE TO ORDER NORA FROM THE MM HERB SHOP

Nettle

contains minerals iron, potassium, calcium, magnesium and copper, as well as vitamin A, C, K, B, chlorophyll and beta carotene. It can balance blood sugar and improve blood flow. For the mamas, nettle prevents postpartum hemorrhage and supports normal lactation.

Oatsraw

supports the nervous system. It contains iron, magnesium, calcium, and vitamin D and E, nourishing the thyroid & aiding in hormone cycling. Oatstraw provides long lasting energy.

Red Raspberry Leaf

is a uterine tonic for healthy menstruation, labor preparation and postpartum healing. RRL may ease pain from cramps. It include vitamins A, B1, B2, and B3 as well as vitamins C and E, manganese, niacin, selenium, magnesium, calcium and iron.

Alfalfa

promotes healthy blood building, supports digestion, and balances blood sugar. It can lower blood pressure, cholesterol, and lessen inflammation and pain.

MINDFULNESS

How our Thoughts, Feelings and Wellbeing are Connected

by Claire Schembri

Did You Know
that each thought is accompanied by a feeling, and every feeling carries a vibration? These vibrations can significantly impact our energy levels and overall wellness. Occasionally, life can be overwhelming, and our energy can become bogged down. As a Certified Vibroacoustic Therapist and Sound Bath practitioner, I understand the importance of addressing negative energy before it builds up and takes a toll on our energy levels, leaving us feeling distracted and confused.

Sedona Desert Dreams

When energy is low, there is potential to get caught in a loop of "fight-or-flight"

The main goal is to get out of the sympathetic nervous system and allow the body and mind to enter the restful parasympathetic system. Healing only takes place in this restful state.

Here is an exercise to practice being still and present. This exercise helps connect the right and left sides of the brain. Give it a try today and be patient with yourself.

Step 1: Choose something to focus on. This can be a person, object, pet, friend or feeling.

Step 2: Ask yourself the following two questions:

When I look at you, what do I see?
When I look at you, what do I feel?

Once you've answered these questions, turn them around and ask yourself the same two questions:

When I look at me, what do I see?
When I look at me, what do I feel?

Using this technique can enhance mindfulness and self-awareness. One of the most satisfying things about self-reflection is the chance to identify where we can improve. By acknowledging shortcomings and utilizing the insights gained from reflection, we can shed our old skin and start anew. Take this opportunity to gain clarity on your inner thoughts and emotions. Once they are acknowledged and understood, they can be released. This creates space for personal growth and allows us to move forward. When we embrace our emotions and allow them to flow through us it allows us to let go of negative energy. Through awareness, forgiveness, and other techniques, we can transform our emotions into positive energy, resulting in an overall lighter and healthier disposition.

Emi Fujii | Sedona Desert Dreams | @sedonadesertdreams

"THE FIRST WORD THAT COMES TO MIND WHEN I THINK OF MY BIRTHING EXPERIENCE IS: EMPOWERING..."

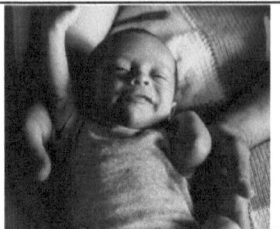
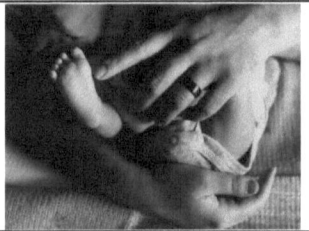
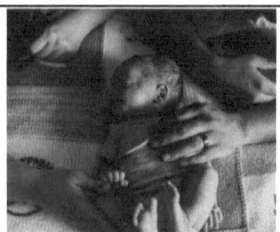

A NICU JOURNEY

Yet, the first seven months after giving birth, I would only think of the words: **Traumatic and Devastating.**

Like a lot of women, I had imagined the *"perfect birth"* of my son. I was ready to wait as long as he wanted before he came earth side, but at 32 weeks pregnant my blood pressure spiked. I was thrown for a loop when a doctor informed me that I had pre-eclampsia, and I was going to be *induced.*

I started to black out with each contraction as they got more and more intense. Shortly after I started pushing, several nurses and doctors came into the room. No one would give me a straight answer as to what was going on, other than the fact that I needed an *emergency c-section.* During the chaos, my husband was left outside of the operating room. I vaguely remember yelling and asking where my husband was,

BUT NO ONE GOT HIM FOR ME…

A doctor ended up holding my hand to calm me down. I later learned that it was the anesthesiologist. He said that I was going to feel a "tug" when they made the incision, but *I felt everything.* Feeling them cut me open is the only thing I can distinctly remember from the operating room, besides wondering if my son was breathing. After that, everything went black. The anesthesiologist decided to put me to sleep, so that I would stop panicking. After 76 hours of labor, my son was finally born.

Waking up in Recovery and Postpartum without your baby really feels hollow and empty. The NICU journey was two weeks- the longest two weeks for a first time parent. My husband and I would visit him everyday, but because of the pandemic, we weren't even able to hold our son. Telling a new mother that she can't hold her baby is not natural. I don't wish that pain on anyone.

We knew there was a light at the end of the tunnel, but the journey was dark. The only saving grace was knowing that each day our son was getting stronger and stronger. *He is our NICU warrior.*

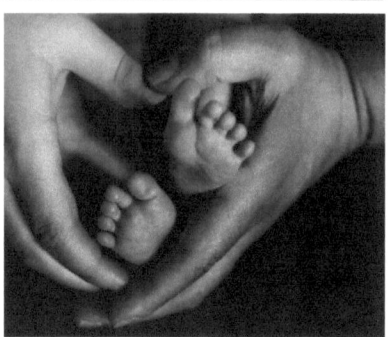

The healing that I had to endure was a long process. I had **rage** towards my husband and newborn baby, then would cry out of **guilt** afterwards. I had constant **fears** of some catastrophic event killing my whole family, and even worse thoughts that I might hurt my own family. I came to terms that I needed to figure out how to help myself. I found a therapist and we worked together for three months to help me process my birth story and even some childhood trauma that was showing up in my postpartum phase.

My birth story opened my eyes to how terrible the system is, as a whole. I'm currently in the process of becoming a postpartum doula because I'm inspired to be there for other women. We need to start the discussions to help the mothers in this society that does not cherish mothers. **It's time to change the narrative.**

-SARAH BYER-

SARAHB.POSTPARTUMDOULA@GMAIL.COM

Golden Goddess Soup

by Victoria Rodomista

For the Soup:
- 1 tablespoon olive oil
- 1/2 white onion (chopped)
- 2 cloves garlic (minced)
- 1 small head cauliflower (rough chop into bite-sized pieces)
- Pinch of cayenne pepper
- 1 tablespoon ground turmeric
- 4 cups unsweetened coconut milk
- 1 teaspoon sea salt (to taste)
- 1 tablespoon FRESH lemon juice
- Freshly ground black pepper
- 1/2 cup fresh basil leaves (finely chopped)
- Curried Chickpea Croutons
- Coconut milk for garnishing (optional)

For Chickpea Croutons:
- 1 can chickpeas (15oz)
- 1 tablespoon curry powder
- 1 tablespoon olive oil
- 1 tablespoon gluten free tamari sauce (or soy sauce if that's your jam!)
- Pinch of salt

The Recipe:

- Heat oil in a large soup pot over medium heat. When oil is shimmering, add onion, garlic, cauliflower, cayenne, and turmeric. Cook 10 minutes, or until fragrant- cauliflower will be a gorgeous golden color!
- Add half of the coconut milk and 1 tsp of salt, bring to a simmer, and simmer until cauliflower softens, around 10 minutes.
- Transfer soup to a blender and blend to a creamy consistency (add more coconut milk if you want it "soupier") *I blend with an immersion blender and it works great.*
- Return soup to the pot, over medium heat and gradually add more coconut milk until you reach your desired consistency. Simmer for 4-5 more minutes.
- Add lemon juice and additional salt and black pepper to taste and serve garnished with the basil, chickpea croutons, a drizzle of coconut milk, if using!

Curried Chickpea Croutons:
- Preheat oven to 400 ˚F.
- Line a baking sheet with parchment paper.
- Drain and rinse chickpeas. Pat dry with paper towels.
- In a bowl, combine chickpeas, curry powder, olive oil, tamari and salt.
- Toss to coat.
- Spread in an even layer on prepared baking sheet and roast 30 minutes, stirring every 10 minutes, until the chickpeas look toasted.

I have a strong passion for cooking- and all things food! I had the opportunity to attend New Orleans Center for Creative Arts and study Culinary Arts thanks to the Emeril Lagasse Foundation."

BLACKBERRY JAM

with Victoria

INGREDIENTS:
-2 pounds organic blackberries
-1.5 cups white sugar
-2.5 tablespoons pectin
-1/2 lemon, juiced

Directions

- Mash blackberries (using a potato masher or something similar) in a medium-heavy based pan, add sugar, berries, lemon, and pectin.

- Heat on low-medium heat, stirring constantly. (This helps avoid crystallized sugar.)

- Increase heat to high, and bring the mixture to a boil (one that can't be stirred down) and let it roar for 5 minutes!

- Reduce heat to simmer, and stir.

- Use a spoon to scrape the foam off the top.

- **Saucer Test** Scoop a spoonful of jam onto a cold plate and wait 30 seconds. If you can move it with your finger and it wrinkles (even a little, you know it will set!) you are now ready for canning!

A Labor of Love

Jam is a labor of love to preserve the sweetness of summer and prepare the mind and body for an introspective winter. Hands-on meditations like cooking are great if you are feeling restless! Cooking and working with food can be a form of meditation, and it is proven to increase happiness, improve focus, and increase overall satisfaction with life while reducing stress and irritability. The finished product also makes the most heartwarming and intentional gifts for your loved ones.

-VICTORIA RODOMISTA

SCAN THE QR CODE FOR A CANNING TUTORIAL

Eulogy of Me

My name is Jennifer Wendy Ramos, and I died Monday, October 4th of 2021.

I lost my husband that day.
He's not missing, he's dead. And on that day, I died too. It was no ordinary day, you see, for I knew he was leaving me.

I could feel his life force energy fading.

The night before his death, I remember speaking with my dearest friend. I could feel this unusual pull toward a future, which challenged me. I wanted to cling to the familiar. I could feel my soul awakening, a shift to a new beginning. I cried to my friend, expressing my fears. Maybe I was wrong about my purpose here. It felt like a choice needed to be made about the fate of my future. But I felt so uncertain; am I coming or going?...

By the next day, the fate of my future hung in the balance. A weird sort of justice played out that day. The scales had turned. All the fears and anguish disappeared, just like an apparition. *I watched my husband's life leave his eyes.* There was a sensing, a deep dark knowing, like this is how it's meant to be. *But why?* On this day, the gift of a sixth sense felt more like a curse.

I have died many times before. But not like this. This death feels like a crucifixion; a cruel and unusual understanding of suffering, from which I know I must rise again. Like the phoenix, reincarnating into a new bird. There's no singular event that has occurred that made me who I am today, but a succession of themes, like seasons, that have orchestrated my path. Life has held no punches, and as I've leaned in, I've felt my power grow. **A strength I didn't even know, began to show.**

This cycle is changing me beyond a physical being. It's the same energy, a sensing, a deep dark knowing, like this is how it's meant to be.

There's always hidden meanings in tragedy, if we are open to receive. We are vessels to the divine. I didn't know it then, but my soul was awakening for yet another time. This journey has brought to me an abundance of gifts to share, from my very own strengths through the struggles I bare.

Losing my husband was the hardest thing I have ever gone through. A complete annihilation of who I was. An opportunity to take all that love and give it to myself. To feed my passion, and walk my purpose, I believe he had to go, and that was always the way it was going to be.

SCAN THE QR CODE TO
VISIT JENNIFER'S WEBSITE

Seven Breaths
with Sharissa Bradley

Spiritual Summer Camp 2023
Smoke Ceremony with Sharissa
Tia Esther Photography

Learn More
from Sharissa

The Origin of 'Seven Breaths'

During a time where native tribes were suffering from droughts and therefore lack of food a beautiful ceremony was presented as a way to give thanks to the land, animals and the tribe. This ceremony was credited for increasing bountiful harvests and creating more harmony in the community. Originally adapted from the book Return of The Bird Tribes, written by Ken Carey, comes the traditional smoke ceremony as performed by The White Buffalo Calf Woman. Although it is now easier to find a way to a grocery store for food and water, it is my belief that a daily ceremony could truly benefit us all. This is an adapted version of the original smoke ceremony that can be used in daily practice and only takes a few moments. This whole process can be done silently in your head. The smoke ceremony, as detailed in Return of the Bird Tribes, included a special pipe and special tobacco grown and blessed for this ceremony. I believe the smoke was used to show the impact that breath makes on the environment. The simplest example of this is when it is cold outside the breath is visible and can be easily seen outside the body. In the absence of cold, to show where the breath is moving once outside the body, smoke can be used. If smoking is already a ritual that exists in your daily life, this short practice can be added to your current routine. If not, burning some herbs or a candle during this practice can be useful in showing exactly how powerful breath can be. Of course, if no smoke is preferred, simply listen to your breath during each exhale. Listen to the blessings leave your body in the form of your breath. If smoke is your chosen method, simply allow the smoke from your chosen source to billow, on each exhalation allow the breath to pass through the smoke. When you leave this practice, after your final smoke exhalation, know that you can take this with you wherever you go. The smoke is only there to show how far the blessings go after leaving your lungs.

The Ceremony

Take a moment to allow your breaths to become as long and as loud as you can, like a loud sigh. Do this for a few breaths until every exhale is at least 5 seconds and audible.
On each inhale imagine each of the seven prompts. On the exhale say thank you to each and watch as the breath is carried on.

01 On the first **inhale** imagine your Great Spirit. This can be the Universe, God, Source, your Highest Self, or the Planet itself. It could also be your thoughts, prayers, or aspirations. On your **exhale** imagine yourself saying thank you.

02 On your second **inhale**, imagine Mother Earth in the form of the earth, sky, and world we live in. On your **exhale** imagine yourself saying thank you.

03 On your third **inhale**, imagine all animals who live on this planet alongside us. On your **exhale** imagine yourself saying thank you.

04 On your fourth **inhale**, imagine your tribe in the form of your family, friends, and support system. On your **exhale** imagine yourself saying thank you.

05 On your fifth **inhale**, imagine the four directions. On your **exhale** imagine yourself saying thank you.

06 On your sixth **inhale**, imagine three people in your life that you would love to bless. On your **exhale** imagine seeing those three people blessed in the exact way only you could.

07 On your final **inhale**, imagine yourself, your body, and your only true home. On your **exhale** imagine yourself saying thank you.

Some Smoking Alternatives:
candle, rosemary, sustainably sourced sage or palo santo, various resin on charcoal

Smoke Cleansing
Herbs & Uses

PALO SANTO
- Purify space, people & objects
- Supports immune system
- Natural insect repellant
- Deeper connection to source
- Eliminates negative energy

SWEETGRASS
- Drive away negative energies
- Cleanse bodies and objects
- Elicit pleasant dreams
- Connect to the spirit world
- Stimulate love and harmony

MUGWORT
- Activates the third eye chakra
- Opens the subconscious
- Stimulates imagination
- Detoxifies the body
- Relieves stress and anxiety

CEDAR
- Promote peaceful thoughts
- Interpret spiritual messages
- Physical & spiritual safeguard
- Increase courage
- Grounding energies

THYME
- Brings courage and confidence
- Mends broken spirits
- Cleanse space and self
- Settle disputes and arguments
- Mental clarity

LAVENDER
- Soothes emotions & stress
- Purifies the air
- Sets a relaxing ambiance
- Induces good sleep
- Removes allergens in the air

ROSE
- Associated with Isis and Venus
- Assists with unconditional love
- Enhance your spiritual skills
- Protective properties
- Balances mood

EUCALYPTUS
- Assists with respiratory issues
- Purifies the air
- Brings mental clarity & peace
- Energizes the mind, body & spirit

SAGE
- Remove bacteria, fungi, and viruses from the air
- Repel insects
- Truth seeker & ancestral work
- Reduce stress and anxiety

BAY LEAVES
- Reduces anxiety
- Improves focus and alertness
- Antibiotic and antiseptic
- Calming
- Brings awareness

-Vivianna, Wild Raven

The Science and Magic of
Reishi Mushrooms

by Nourish the Mama

For centuries, reishi mushrooms have been used in traditional Chinese medicine as a powerful healing herb. Reishi is prized for its ability to support the immune system, reduce stress and anxiety, and even promote longevity. Recently, they seem to be enjoying a resurgence of recognition for the profound role they can play in our health — physically, mentally, and spiritually.

What exactly can reishi mushrooms do for your health and well-being?

Reishi mushrooms are immune-modulating, meaning they have the ability to increase or decrease the immune function depending on what is needed. Some studies have shown that reishi mushrooms may be beneficial for people with high blood pressure and/or high cholesterol, as they have been shown to improve circulation and reduce inflammation in the body. Reishi tinctures can also help support a healthy sleep cycle.

Makenna D Photography

Reishi Tincture

Mushroom of Immortality

Dosage: 1 dropperful twice daily

Triple Extraction Method
Ingredients: organic reishi, alcohol, water, non-GMO organic glycerin, raw local honey

Reishi Babies

"Reishi Baby" is a term to describe babies that are born to mamas who have consumed reishi mushrooms consistently during their pregnancies. The calming qualities it imbues on the emotions and nervous system are seemingly passed onto the baby. It has been noted that these "Reishi Babies" appear to be calm, peaceful and alert, and seem to be "buddha-like". Ron Teeguarden is a master herbalist, known for bringing herbalism to the United States. He stated that Reishi Babies appeared uniformly calm and focused, had little or no inflammation, cried little, and appeared to take in their surroundings with incredible acuity.

For "Reishi Babies", this tincture is ideally started before pregnancy, consistently used throughout the pregnancy and while nursing. Consistency is key—whether pregnant or otherwise—as it allows the full benefits of reishi to be utilized.

Consuming Reishi

As far as dosage, 1-2ml (1-2 dropper-fuls) a day is generally a good place to start. To get the maximum benefit from your reishi mushroom tincture, consider adding it to your morning or evening routine. You can take reishi whenever you need a little extra support. However, reishi has the ability to adapt to the changing needs of your system and allows issues to be addressed before symptoms arise. Taking it consistently allows the full benefits of reishi to be experienced. Be patient, as it may take several weeks or even months before you start to notice the full benefits of your reishi mushroom tincture.

Sourcing Reishi

It's important to choose a handcrafted small batch apothecary for the best quality. When it comes to herbal remedies, quality matters. Look for an apothecary who uses organic or wild harvested reishi mushrooms. Some of the best quality reishi mushrooms come from China where farming practices have been passed down for generations.

@makennadphotography

SCAN THE
QR CODE
TO VISIT
NOURISH
THE MAMA

Freedom from Diagnosis:
MUSHROOMS, MINERALS, AND MUSCLES

By Alyssa VanDerLinden

Growing up I did well in school but was often told that I talked too much or that I wasn't living up to my potential. I also had a hard time fitting in and often felt different and alone. In high school I started using alcohol as a coping mechanism. I thought it would help me "fit in" and be more comfortable in social situations but it never did. I did not know how to connect with people and found myself oversharing often and always left filled with regret.

Entering into adulthood I was still using my failing coping strategies all while navigating being a wife and mom trying to "do it all" while constantly feeling like I was drowning. I was overweight, depressed and ready for a change. I decided to finally quit drinking in January of 2022 and my life began quickly improving. I was exercising daily and focusing on nutrition. Social media was my go-to spot for finding helpful information to improve my fitness and nutrition. Soon I found myself researching ADHD on social media. Educators were sharing about facets of neurodivergence that I had never heard before like addiction, body image issues, rejection sensitivity dysphoria (RSD), impulsivity, organizational issues, time blindness, depression, anxiety and so much more. Each post I saw I felt like it was made just for me. As if someone knew all my private thoughts. It took about a week for me to fully connect the dots and diagnose myself with ADHD.

This diagnosis explained so much. I was relieved to finally know why I always felt so alone and different. It also explained why simple everyday things felt much harder for me than those around me. However, the relief that came with the diagnosis quickly turned into grief. All I could think about was what my life could have been had I known sooner and had the help I desperately needed. How many huge life mistakes could I have avoided? How much happier I could have been for all those years. It took at least two months for me to come to terms with my diagnosis and try to let go of the feelings of "what could have been". During that time, I started connecting more dots, seeing a connection in my family members and their potential neurodivergence. I have lost several family members to drug overdoses, alcoholism and suicide, all of which are more likely in neurodivergent populations. I began thinking about all these undiagnosed people in my life that, if diagnosed and given the proper help, could still be here. It was heartbreaking.

Shortly after coming to terms with the ADHD diagnoses I was researching natural remedies to help alleviate ADHD symptoms. I learned that ADHD is closely related to Dopamine levels. Those with ADHD often find dopamine in unhealthy and dangerous situations that involve excessive alcohol, drugs or casual sex. These types of behaviors can result in addiction issues and self-harm. I was on a mission to find a natural alternative treatment for ADHD. In my search, I found what I call the three M's: Mushrooms, Minerals and Muscles.

I finally feel at home in my body and the more I learn about how my brain works the more comfortable I am feeling in my mind. I know I have a long journey ahead, but I am so grateful to all the wonderful people that put themselves out there for all the world to see, ADHD warts and all! Now I feel like it's my turn to help as many people as possible, especially women because we have a far greater issue with misdiagnosis and medical gas lighting along with ever climbing societal expectations. We women need to really focus on nourishing our bodies and honoring ourselves. As I tell my clients we are the only ones who can take care of ourselves, and we deserve it! *Love yourself* and never stop growing.

Photo of Victoria Rodomista by Tia Esther Creative

"I finally feel at home in my body."

The Three *Ms*

Mushrooms

Following a family member's attempted suicide and a miscarriage, I found myself in the depths of depression. On a Monday morning, I woke up ready to die. I knew it was time for a change. I took a microdose of psilocybin that morning. That evening as I laid in bed tears of joy and gratitude were rolling down my face. I was grateful to be alive. I could finally see everything that was good in my life. These results have been lasting and I truly feel like my brain has been changed for the better and was rewired for positivity. Aside from psilocybin, some functional mushrooms like lion's mane, reishi, chaga and cordyceps have also been shown to help ADHD symptoms.

Minerals

Most people find themselves mineral deficient, especially mothers. A woman can lose approximately 3 lbs. of minerals during pregnancy alone. Simply adding a pinch of raw Himalayan pink salt to your water can make a wonderful change to your hydration and mineral levels. I personally experienced the most dramatic results from Fulvic and Humic acid which allowed me to pass parasites and mucoid plaque that had created devastating effects on my digestive system and health as a whole. Research now shows that Dopamine is primarily made in the gut. It is important to support gut health in any way possible.

Muscle

Weight training has been instrumental in boosting my self-confidence by aiding in weight loss and building a body I am proud of. It has also shown me that I can do hard things! I have been able to see the progress as each month I am able to lift heavier than I did the month before. Of course, the extra endorphins don't hurt either. Showing up for myself everyday and doing the hard work of true self care has been the ultimate show of self-love. While also being a great role model for my son. Hearing him cheer me on and saying, "Wow mom, you're strong!" has been such a rewarding experience in itself. Now, I find myself going from wanting to be the smallest person in the room to wanting to be the strongest. Not just physically but mentally and spiritually.

MISS JAMIE GREEN'S
SALMON WELLINGTON

With Spinach and

Cream Cheese Filling

@miss_jamie_green
_____
Yield: 2-4 Servings

INGREDIENTS

- 2 salmon filets, skinless
- 1 tsp salt
- 1/2 tsp pepper
- 1/8 tsp garlic powder
- 2 tbsp butter
- 2 large cloves, diced
- 1 cup yellow onion, diced
- 5 cups spinach, roughly chopped
- 1/3 cup breadcrumbs, (no extra flavor)
- 4 oz cream cheese
- ¼ parmesan cheese,
- 2 tbsp fresh dill
- 2 sheets puff pastry, thawed
- 1 egg, beaten

PROCEDURE

1. Preheat oven to 425 °F.
2. Line baking sheet with parchment paper.
3. Sprinkle salt, pepper (or lemon pepper) and garlic powder on both sides of the salon filets and set aside.
4. In a large skillet over medium heat, melt the butter. Add the diced onions and cook until translucent. Add the garlic, stirring constantly, continue cooking until onions stand garlic start to brown. Do not let the garlic burn.
5. Add the spinach, salt and pepper, and cook until spinach is slightly wilted but still bright green.
6. Add the cream cheese first and allow it to start to melt, sprinkle in breadcrumbs, parmesan cheese. Keep stirring mixture until the cream cheese has fully melted and all ingredients are evenly combined. Stir in dill last. Remove from heat and set aside.
7. Use a cutting board, or parchment paper, lay one sheet of puff pastry flat and use your hands to smooth out the folds. Place one salmon filet in the center.

8. Place half the spinach mixture on top of the filet, smoothing it out over the length of the filet, careful not to let it spill over the sides. Mixture should only be on top of the filet.
9. Fold the edges of the puff pastry over the salmon and spinach mixture, starting with the longer sides and the shorter ones. Dab a little water with your finger on the edges of the pasty to help it stick shut. Trim off any excess puff pastry. Flip the pastry pocket over so that the seam is on the bottom.
10. Repeat steps for the second filet.
11. Brush the beaten egg over the tops of the pastry pockets. Using a knife, score the top of the pastry in a crosshatch pattern making sure to cut only through the pastry and not the salmon. Similar to a pie, these cuts are to release the steam that can get trapped inside. Plus, it looks pretty. Brush a second coat of egg across the top.
12. Bake for 20-25 minutes, or until the pastry is golden brown.

PROUD TO BE
CRONE

BY PAMELA BUEHL

The image of a crone is of an older lady sitting all alone.
She is withered away with beauty faded to none.
This is not my story from maiden to mother to crone.
My path has been a wild and wonderful journey that started in 1961!

As a maiden, I was fun and carefree.
Life was gentle and easy, not burdened by expectation and "role".
I was exploring what it was to be me.
Living was free and had not taken a toll.
Motherhood came when I was fairly young.
Anticipating my first sweet child, It didn't matter, girl or boy.
I felt strong and proud, a new stage had begun.
I was not prepared for sleepless nights, body changes, or such sweet joy!
Motherhood brought out a strength and force I didn't know was inside.
Experienced mothers loved and guided me along the way.
Watching my little humans grow brought so much pride.
Enjoy the little moments, the experienced mommas would say.
Raising them up, at the moment, seems to take so long.
Then, the conflicts arise when they want to be free.
How quickly they fly from their nest and join their friends in song.
With tears, I see my parenting success, as they prepare to leave me!
Life continues and family dynamics ebb and flow.
My children, now adults, have moved on with their life.
I proudly watch as they choose the directions they will go.
Then, a shifting takes place, refocusing as husband and wife.
At the ripe "old age" of 61, I would now be considered a crone.
Age is just a label, I have much more life to live.
I feel the re-awakening of the maiden once known.
Along your path, seek the crones in your life, we are so ready to give!

A Year in Poetry by Pamela Buehl

SCAN THE QR CODE
FOR A FREE PREVIEW

LARA & JESSE ST JAMES
TIA ESTHER CREATIVE

SPICE UP YOUR FALL

Tia Esther Photography

"I love the Fall cozy vibes, pumpkin spice, and seasonal treats. But.. Fall also brings unpleasant ailments. Fortunately, Ayurveda has some delicious and immune-boosting recipes that can help you stay healthy through the season."

by Tanya Murguia

1 GINGER TURMERIC TEA

This classic golden elixir is a powerhouse of anti-inflammatory and immune-boosting properties.
Simply boil a cup of water, add a tablespoon of grated ginger and a teaspoon of turmeric powder, and let it steep for 5-10 minutes. Sweeten with honey or maple syrup if desired.

2 SPICED APPLE OATMEAL

A warm bowl of oatmeal and spiced apple is the perfect way to start your day.
Cook your oats as usual, then add diced apples, cinnamon, nutmeg, and a pinch of cardamom. Top with a drizzle of maple syrup and some chopped nuts for extra flavor and crunch.

3 SQUASH + LENTIL SOUP

Seasonal squash with the protein and fiber of lentils is a yummy balanced meal.
Sauté some onion and garlic in a pot, then add cubed squash, red lentils, vegetable broth, and your favorite spices (we like cumin, coriander, and smoked paprika). Let it simmer until everything is tender, then blend until smooth for a creamy and satisfying soup.

4 ROASTED BRUSSELS SPROUTS WITH MUSTARD VINAIGRETTE

Not everyone's favorite vegetable, but roasting them brings out their natural sweetness and adds a crispy texture.
Toss halved sprouts with olive oil, salt, and pepper, then roast in the oven until golden brown. Meanwhile, whisk together some dijon mustard, apple cider vinegar, and maple syrup for a tangy and sweet vinaigrette. Drizzle over the roasted sprouts and enjoy as a side dish or snack.

5 GOLDEN MILK LATTE

The ultimate fall beverage: golden milk latte
Heat up a cup of coconut milk with turmeric, ginger, cinnamon, and a pinch of black pepper (to aid in turmeric absorption), then blend until frothy. Sweeten with honey or maple syrup and savor every sip.
These spicy fall recipes are sure to hit the spot this season and keep you balanced and happy. Need more tips this fall? Contact me as your ayurvedic coach for more guidance.

NOURISH   RENEW

FALL CHAI RECIPES

Chai Spiced Sautéed Apples in Ghee

@UNCONDITIONALLY.ALICIA

Makes Two Servings

- 2 Apples, diced
- 1 tbsp maple syrup
- 1 tbsp grassfed ghee
- 1/2 tsp cinnamon
- 1/4 tsp ground cardamom
- 1/4 tsp ground nutmeg
- 1/4 tsp ground ginger
- Pinch of ground clove

1. Mix spices and set aside.
2. Heat ghee in sauté pan on medium heat.
3. Once warm add apples and maple syrup.
4. Once apples begin to soften add spices.
5. Sauté until golden brown and carmelized to your liking. 5-10 mins.
6. Remove from the heat and enjoy! Can be used as a topping for oatmeal, yogurt, etc. or can be enjoyed by themselves.

Bullet Chai Tea

@ALISHACMEYER

- 1 steeped 8 oz cup of chai tea
- 1 tbsp coconut oil or butter
- Splash of Milk of choice
- Scoop of collagen
- Maple Syrup to taste
- Add everything to a blender and enjoy!

The Wheel of your Soul

Past Lives as Seasons and Your Own Changing Experience

by Liana Soria

Remembering your past lives is a deep and powerful way to get to know yourself.

As a past life therapist, I would say that you can't know who you truly are without some significant past life memories. Here's a concept I like to discuss: If you clearly access memories from one other past life, you can compare it to your life now. All the differences in personality, assumptions, and values can then be seen as a result of culture, time, and upbringing, for example. Then it's fair to say that what is the same in both lifetimes is probably a characteristic of the soul, and of your unchanging qualities. This is already so much self-awareness, but if you continue to gather memories of *more lifetimes* you will have more and more aspects of yourself, known to be conditioning, as well as more unchanging soul qualities. These unchanging qualities make up your True Self, your soul.

Thinking of yourself as your soul, instead of as your individual personality, circumstances, or body, produces an interesting shift. You begin to see yourself as moving through life, and indeed lifetimes, for development. These deepening experiences seem to dig little grooves into your soul, forming unique patterns found nowhere else. So even seemingly negative experiences, or challenges that come again and again have a positive aspect. They're yours and you wouldn't be you without them.

Your past life stories are your story.

In the Spring and Summer of your soul, you're building a sense of yourself, and often learn through a lot of trial and error. In the Autumn and Winter lifetimes and times of life, you gain a sense of what you're not. This allows you to identify and remove blocks, easily let go of karma, and spend more time in alignment with your truth. As you remember who you really are, you will experience a deepening realization of the cyclical nature of all situations. Now, when in difficulty, you know it's temporary and can relax in situations that would have been impossible for you to relax in before. You seem wise to others. Now, as you navigate the most important lifetime, the life you're living now, feel where you are. In what aspects are you young, still building something, still learning? Seek out mentors that already have the results you want for yourself. Now, what comes easily to you, what can you do that seems so simple and obvious to you that you feel a little shy to present it as talent, or as a gift? These are the mastered elements of your soul, and it's time to share those freely with others. And stay humble, because the gifts of your soul came from long experience, long long experience.

May the cycles and seasons of your soul be blessed for all time.